A Scolar Press Facsimile

DIANA

Henry Constable
[1594]

Printed and published in Great Britain by
The Scolar Press Limited, Menston, Yorkshire
and 39 Great Russell Street, London WC1

This facsimile first published 1973

ISBN
0 85417 988 7

Introductory note

Henry Constable (1562–1613) enjoyed a secure reputation in his own time as an admired writer of sonnets on the Italian model. His indebtedness to Sidney is seen not only in his dedications of individual poems but in a shared adherence to the Continental pattern and to such specific predecessors as Philippe Desportes, whose *Diane* provided Constable with a title for his own collection. Claims have been made for his direct influence on the sonnets of Daniel, Drayton, and Shakespeare, as well as such lesser figures as Barnes and Barnfield. In an ode in *Under-wood*, Jonson praises 'Constables Ambrosiack Muse' and pairs him with Sidney in merit, a judgment shared by Drayton and Gabriel Harvey as well as by later writers.

Though he was formerly known only as an author of secular poetry, today he is recognized as the author of 'Spirituall Sonnettes' which are found in Harleian MS. 7553, and as a Catholic whose religion (as well as his involvement with Essex) had led to his exile to the continent by the time the *Diana* was first published in 1592. Consequently, his sonnets must antedate most of the important English collections, and claim additional respect for this priority.

The edition reproduced here is assigned to 1594 by a tradition which goes back to 1802 (Ritson, *Bibliographia Poetica*); no copy now exists which bears a date, but traces of some date seem to be visible at the trimmed bottom edge of the title page in the British Museum copy (shelf-mark: c.39.a.60). This copy is reproduced here by permission of the Trustees, except for signature F, which the British Museum copy has only in facsimile and is here taken from the copy in the Bodleian, by permission of the Curators (shelf-mark: Malone 436).

The 1592 edition, with the title *DIANA. The praises of his Mistres, in certaine sweete Sonnets* consists of twenty-two sonnets (numbered in Italian), and is extant in two known copies, at Corpus Christi College, Oxford, and the Huntington Library. Like the later edition it seems to have been assembled in Constable's absence, as a prefatory note implies in referring to the poems as 'now by misfortune left as Orphans'. The more enigmatic printer's note in 1594, with its allusion to Aeneas and Turnus, may glance at Constable's possibly controversial position. It is unclear how many poems in this 'augmented' edition are by Constable himself: eight of them are generally recognized as by Sidney, and were included among his *Certain Sonnets* of 1598 (Ringler, ed., *Poems of Sir Philip Sidney*, 1962, CS 1, 2, 8–11, 18, 20). Constable's modern editor, Joan Grundy (1960), bases her text on the Todd manuscript (Victoria and Albert Museum, MS. Dyce 44), which contains a carefully arranged collection of sonnets divided into three groups each with three sets of seven poems, as well as prefatory and concluding remarks on this organization and the resulting 'climatericall number 63'.

Ref.: STC 5638.

DONALD CHENEY

DIANA.

OR,

The excellent conceitful Sonnets
of *H. C.* Augmented with diuers
Quatorzains of honorable and
lerned perſonages.

Deuided into viij. Decads.

Vincitur a facibus, qui iacet ipſe faces.

AT LONDON,
Printed by *Iames Roberts* for
Richard Smith.

THE PRINTER TO
the Reader.

Bſcur'd wonders (gentle-men,) viſited me in *Turnus* armor, and I in regard of *Aeneas* honour, haue vn-clouded them vnto the worlde : you are that Vniuerſe, you that *Aeneas*, if you finde *Pallas* gyrdle, murder them, if not inviron'd vvith barbarizme, ſaue them, and eternitie will prayſe you.

Vale.

A 2

VNTO HER MAIE-
sties sacred honorable
Maydes.

ETernall Twins that conquer Death and Time,
    Perpetuall Aduocates in Heauen and Earth,
    Fayre, chast, imaculat, and all diuine,
        Glorious alone, before the first mans byrth :
    You two-fold CHARITES, celestiall lights,
Bow your Sun-ryfing eyes, Planets of ioy,
Vpon these Orphan Poems : in whose rights,
Conceit first claym'd his byrth-right to enioy.
    If pittifull, you shun the song of Death,
Or feare the staine of Loues life-dropping blood,
O know then you are pure, and purer fayth,
Shall still keepe white, the flower, the fruite, and bud.
    Loue moueth all things, you that loue, shall moue
    All things in him : and he in you shall loue.

                              RICHARD
                                  SMYTH.

The first Decad.

SONNET. I.

REsolu'd to loue, vnworthy to obtaine,
  I doe no fauour craue : but humble wise
  to thee my sighes in verse I sacrifise;
  onely some pitty, and no helpe to gaine.
Heare then, and as my hart shall aye remaine
  a patient obiect to thy lightning eyes :
  a patient eare bring thou to thundring cries;
  feare not the cracke, when I the blow sustaine.
So, as thine eye bred mine ambitious thought,
  so shall thine eare make proud my voyce for ioy :
  lo (Deere) what wonders great by thee are wrought
  when I but little fauours doe enioy.
The voyce is made the eare for to reioyce :
And your eare giueth pleasure to my voyce.
                              B.   Blame

SONNET. II.

B Lame not my hart for flying vp too hie,
  sith thou art cause that it this flight begunne;
  for earthly vapours drawne vp by the Sunne,
  Comets begun, and night-sunnes in the skie.
Mine humble hart, so with thy heauenly eie
  drawne vp aloft, all low desires doth shunne :
  raise then me vp, as thou my hart hast done,
  so during night, in heauen remaine may I.
I say againe, blame not my high desire,
  sith of vs both the cause thereof depends :
  in thee doth shine; in mee doth burne a fire,
  fire drawes vp other, and it selfe ascends.
Thine eye a fire, and so drawes vp my loue :
My loue a fire, and so ascends aboue.

Fly

SONNET. III.

Fly low deere Loue, thy Sunne dooſt thou not ſee?
take heede, doe not ſo neere his rayes aſpyre:
leaſt (for thy pride, inflam'd with wreakful ire)
it burne thy wings, as it hath burned me.
Thou (haply) ſaiſt, thy wings immortall bee,
and ſo cannot conſumed be with fire:
the one is *Hope*, the other is deſire,
and that the heauens beſtow'd them both on thee.
A Muſes words made thee with *Hope* to flye,
an Angels face *Deſire* hath begot,
thy ſelfe engendred by a Goddeſſe eye:
yet for all this, immortall thou art not.
Of heauenly eye though thou begotten art,
Yet art thou borne but of a mortall hart.

B 2   A

SONNET. IIII.

A Friend of mine, pittying my hopelesse loue,
   hoping (by killing hope) my loue to slay :
   Let not (quoth he) thy hope thy hart betray,
   impossible it is her hart to moue.
But sith resolued loue cannot remoue,
   as long as thy diuine perfections stay :
   thy Godhead then he sought to take away.
   Deere seeke reuenge, and him a lyar proue.
Gods onely doe impossibilities,
   impossible (saith he) thy grace to gaine :
   show then the power of thy diuinities,
   by graunting me thy fauour to obtaine.
So shall thy foe giue to himselfe the lie :
A Goddesse thou shalt proue, and happy I.

                                 Thine

SONNET. V.

Thine eye the glaffe where I behold my hart,
  mine eye the window through the which thine eye
  may fee my hart, and there thy felfe efpy
  in bloody cullours how thou painted art.
Thine eye the pyle is of a murdring dart,
  mine eye the fight thou tak'ft thy leuell by
  to hit my hart, and neuer ſhootes awry;
  mine eye thus helpes thine eye to worke my fmart.
Thine eye a fire is both in heate and light,
  mine eye of teares a riuer doth become :
  oh that the water of mine eye had might
  to quench the flames that frõ thine eye doth come.
Or that the fire kindled by thine eye,
The flowing ſtreames of mine eyes could make drie.

B 3   Mine

SONNET. VI.

Mine eye with all the deadly sinnes is fraught,
  1. First *proud*, sith it presum'd to looke so hie :
a watchman being made, stoode gazing by,
  2. and *idle*, tooke no heede till I was caught :
3. And *enuious*, beares enuie that by thought
  should in his absence be to her so nie :
to kill my hart, mine eye let in her eye,
  4. and so consent gaue to a *murther* wrought :
5. And *couetous*, it neuer would remoue
  from her faire haire, gold so doth please his sight :
  6. *Vnchast*, a baude betweene my hart and loue :
  7. a *glutton* eye, with teares drunke euery night.
These sinnes procured haue a Goddesse ire :
Wherfore my hart is damnd in Loues sweet fire.
                        Falslie

SONNET. VII.

FAlſly doth enuie of your praiſes blame
　my tongue, my pen, my hart of flattery :
　becauſe I ſaid there was no ſunne but thee,
　it call'd my tongue the partiall trumpe of Fame ;
And ſaith my pen hath flattered thy name,
　becauſe my pen did to my tongue agree ;
　and that my hart muſt needs a flatrer bee,
　which taught both tongue & pen to ſay the ſame.
No, no, I flatter not, when thee I call
　the ſunne, ſith that the ſunne was neuer ſuch :
　but when the ſunne thee I compar'd withall,
　doubtles the ſunne I flattered too much.
Witnes mine eyes I ſay the truteh in this :
They haue ſeene thee, and know that ſo it is.

Much

SONNET. VIII.

MVch sorrow in it selfe my loue doth moue,
more my dispaire, to loue a hopelesse blisse:
my folly most, to loue whom sure to misse;
oh helpe me but this last greefe to remoue.
All paines if you commaund, it ioy shall proue,
and wisedome to seeke ioy: then say but this;
because my pleasure in thy torment is,
I doe commaund thee without hope to loue.
So, when this thought my sorrow shall augment,
that my owne folly did procure my paine,
then shall I say to giue my selfe content,
obedience onely made me loue in vaine.
It was your will, and not my want of wit:
I haue the paine, beare you the blame of it.

My

SONNET. IX.

MY Ladies presence makes the Roses red,
  because to see her lips, they blush for shame :
  the Lyllies leaues (for enuie) pale became,
  and her white hands in them this enuie bred.
The Marigold the leaues abroad doth spred,
  because the sunnes, and her power is the same :
  the Violet of purple cullour came,
  di'd in the blood shee made my hart to shed.
In briefe, all flowers from her their vertue take ;
  frō her sweet breath, their sweet smels do proceede,
  the liuing heate which her eye beames doth make,
  warmeth the ground, and quickeneth the seede :
The raine wherewith shee watereth the flowers,
Falls from mine eyes, which she dissolues in showers.
                                            Heraulds

SONNET. X.

HEraulds at armes doe three perfections quote,
    to wit, most faire, most ritch, most glittering :
    so when those three concurre within one thing,
    needes must that thing of honor be a note.
Lately I did behold a ritch faire coate,
    which wished Fortune to mine eyes did bring,
    a lordly coate, yet worthy of a King,
    in which one might all these perfections note.
A field of Lyllies, roses proper bare,
    two starres in chiefe, the Crest was waues of gold,
    how glittring twas, might by the starres appeare,
    the Lillies made it faire for to behold.
And ritch it was as by the gold appeareth,
But happy he that in his armes it weareth.

If

The second Decad.

SONNET. I.

IF true loue might true loues reward obtaine,
  dumbe wonder onely might speake of my ioy :
  but too much worth hath made thee too much coy,
  and told me long agoe, I sigh'd in vaine.
Not then vaine hope of vndeserued gaine,
  hath made me paint in verses mine annoy :
  but for thy pleasure, that thou might'st enioy
  thy beauties praise, in glasses of my paine.
See then thy selfe (though me thou wilt not heare)
  by looking on my verse : for paine in verse,
  loue doth in paine, beautie in loue appeare.
  so, if thou wouldst my verses meaning see,
Expound them thus, when I my loue rehearse ;
None loues like him ; that is, None faire like mee.

It

SONNET. II.

IT may be, Loue my death doth not pretend,
   although he shoots at mee : but thinks it fit
   thus to bewitch thee for thy benefit,
   causing thy will to my wish condiscend.
For VVitches which some murther doe intend,
   doe make a picture, and doe shoote at it ;
   and in that part where they the picture hit,
   the parties selfe doth languish to his end.
So Loue too weake by force thy hart to taint,
   within my hart thy heauenly shape doth paint :
   suffring therein his arrowes to abide,
   onely to th'end he might by witches arte,
Within my hart pierce through thy pictures side,
And through thy pictures side might wound my hart.
                                        The

SONNET. III.

THE Sunne his iourney ending in the Weſt,
   taking his lodging vp in *Thetis* bed,
   though from our eyes his beames be baniſhed,
   yet with his light th' *Antipodes* be bleſt.
Now when the ſun-time brings my Sunne to reſt,
   (which mee too oft of reſt hath hindered)
   and whiter skinne with white ſheete couered,
   and ſofter cheeke doth on ſoft pillow reſt :
Then I (oh Sunne of ſunnes, and light of lights)
   wiſh mee with thoſe *Antipodes* to be,
   which ſee and feele thy beames & heate by nights.
   Well though the night both cold and darkſome is,
Yet halfe the dayes delight the night graunts mee :
I feele my Sunnes heate, though his light I miſſe.

                               Lady

SONNET. IIII.

L Adie in beautie and in fauour rare,
  of fauour (not of due) I fauour craue :
  nature to thee Beauty and fauour gaue ;
  faire then thou art, and fauour thou maift fpare.
Nor when on mee beftow'd your fauours are,
  leffe fauour in your face you fhall not haue :
  if fauour then a wounded foule may faue,
  of murthers guilt (deere Lady) then beware.
My loffe of life a million fold were leffe,
  than the leaft loffe fhould vnto you befall :
  yet graunt this gyft, which gift when I poffeffe,
  both I haue life, and you no loffe at all.
For by your Fauor onely I doe liue :
And fauour you may well both keepe and giue.

My

SONNET. V.

MY *Reason* abfent, did mine eyes require
   to watch and ward, and fuch foes to defcrie
as they fhould neere my hart approching fpie :
but traitor eyes my harts death did confpire,
(Corrupted with *Hopes* gyfts) let in *Defire*
   to burne my hart : and fought no remedy,
though ftore of water were in eyther eye ;
which well imployde, might wel haue quencht the
Reafon returnd, *Loue* and *Fortune* made   (fire.
   Iudges, to iudge mine eyes to punifhment :
Fortune, fith they by fight my hart betraid,
from wifhed fight adiudg'd them banifhment :
Loue, fith by fire murdred my hart was found,
Adiudged them in teares for to be drownd.

                             Wonder

SONNET. VI.

WOnder it is, and pittie ift, that shee
    in whom all beauties treasure we may finde,
    that may enrith the body and the mind,
    towards the poore should vse no charitie.
My loue is gone a begging vnto thee,
    and if that Beauty had not beene more kind
    then Pittie, long ere this he had beene pinde :
    but Beautie is content his foode to bee.
Oh pittie haue, when such poore Orphans beg ;
    Loue (naked boy) hath nothing on his backe :
    and though he wanteth neither arme nor leg,
    yet maim'd he is, sith he his sight doth lacke.
And yet (though blinde) he beautie can behold :
And yet (though nak'd) he feeles more heate thã cold.
                           Pittie

SONNET. VII.

Pitty refusing my poore Loue to feede,
a begger staru'd for want of helpe he lies,
and at your mouth (the doore of Beauty) cries,
that thence some almes of sweete grants might pro-
But as he waiteth for some almes-deede,   (ceede.
a cherrie tree before the doore he spies ;
oh deere (quoth he) two cherries may suffise,
two onely may saue life in this my neede.
But beggers, can they naught but cherries eate ?
Pardon my Loue, he is a Goddesse sonne,
and neuer feedeth but on daintie meate,
els neede he not to pine as hee hath done :
For onely the sweet fruite of this sweete tree,
Can giue foode to my Loue, and life to mee.
                                     C.   The

SONNET. VIII.

THE Fouler hides (as closely as he may)
  the net, where caught the sillie bird should be,
  least he the threatning pryson should but see,
  and so for feare be forc'd to flye away.
My Lady so, the while shee doth assay
  in curled knots fast to entangle me,
  put on her vaile, to th'end I should not flee
  the golden net, wherein I am a pray.
Alas (most sweet) what neede is of a net,
  to catch a byrd, that is already tane?
  Sith with your hand alone you may it get,
  for it desires to flie into the same.
What neede such arte, my thoughts then to intrap :
When of themselues they flye into your lap.

                                    Sweet

SONNET. IX.

Sweet hand the sweet, but cruell bowe thou art,
  from whence at mee fiue yuorie arrowes flie :
  so with fiue woundes at once I wounded lie,
  bearing my brest the print of euery dart.
Saint *Fraunces* had the like, yet felt no smart ;
  where I in liuing torments neuer die :
  his woundes were in his hands and feete, where I
  all these fiue helplesse wounds feele in my hart.
Now (as Saint *Fraunces*) if a Saint am I,
  the bowe that shot these shafts a relique is :
  I meane the hand, which is the reason why
  so many for deuotion thee would kisse :
And some thy gloue kisse, as a thing diuine,
This arrowes quiuer, and this reliques shrine.

C 2

Faire

SONNET. X.

Faire Sunne, if you wold haue me praise your light,
  when night approcheth, wherfore doe you flie?
  Time is so short, Beauties so many be,
  as I haue neede to see them day and night:
That by continuall view, my verses might
  tell all the beames of your diuinitie;
  which praise to you, and ioy should be to mee,
  you liuing by my verse, I by your sight.
I by your sight, and not you by my verse:
  neede mortall skill immortall praise rehearse?
  no, no, though eyes were blind, & verse were dumb,
  your beautie shold be seene, & your fame known.
For by the winde which from my sighes doe come,
Your praises round about the world is blowne.

                              The

The third Decad.

SONNET. I.

VNciuill sicknesse, hast thou no regard,
  but doost presume my deerest to molest?
and without leaue dar'st enter in that brest,
whereto sweet Loue approch yet neuer dar'd?
Spare thou her health, which my life hath not spar'd,
  too bitter such reuenge of my vnrest :   (prest,
although with wrongs my thought shee hath op-
  my wrongs seeke not reuenge, they craue reward.
Cease Sicknesse, cease in her then to remaine,
  and come and welcome, harbour thou in me :
who Loue long since hath taught to suffer paine.
So shee which hath so oft my paine increast,
(Oh God, that I might so reuenged be,)
By my poore paine, might haue her paine releast.

C 3   The

SONNET. II.

THe scourge of life, & deathes extreame disgrace,
 the smoake of hell, that monster called paine,
 long shamd to be accurst in euery place,
 by them who of his rude resort complaine :
Like catife wretch by time and trauell taught,
 his ougly ills in others good to hide,
 lateharbours in her face, whom nature wrought
 as treasure house where her best gifts abide.
And so by priuiledge of sacred seate,
 (a seate where beauty shines, and vertue raignes,)
 he hopes for some smal praise, since she hath great,
 within her beames wrapping his cruel staines.
Ah saucie Paine, let not thine error last,
More louing eyes shee drawes, more hate thou hast.
         Woe

SONNET. III.

Woe, woe to me, on mee returne the smart,
  my burning tongue hath bred my Mistres paine,
for oft in paine to paine my painfull hart
with her due praise, didst of my state complaine.
I prais'd her eyes whom neuer change doth moue,
  her breath, which makes a sower aunswere sweet,
her milken breasts, the nurse of child-like loue,
her legs (ô legs) her day well-stepping feete.
Paine heard her praise, and full of inward fire,
  first sayling vp my hart (as pray of his)
hee flyes to her and boldned with desire,
her face (this ages praise) the theefe doth kisse.
O Paine, I now recant the praise I gaue,
And sweare shee is not worthy thee to haue.

                                   Thou

SONNET. IIII.

THou paine, the one:y guest of loath'd constraint,
 the child of curffe, mans weakenes foster child,
 brother to woe, and Father of complaint,
 thou paine, thou lothed paine frō heauen exilde :
How hold'st ẙ her whose eies constraint doth feare,
 whò curst,doth blesse,who weakneth vertues arme,
 who others woes and plaints can chastly heare,
 in whose sweet heauē,angels of hie thoughts swarm
What courage strange hath caught thy catife hart ?
 Fear'st not a.face that oft whole harts deuours ?
 or art thou from aboue byd play this part?
 and so no helpe gainst enuie of those powers.
If thus, alas ; yet whilst those parts haue wo,
So stay her tongue that shee no more say no.

         And

SONNET. V.

AND haue I heard her say, ô cruell paine,
    and doth she know what mould her beuty beares
    mournes shee in troth, & thinks that others faine?
    feares shee to feele, and feeles not others feares?
O doth she thinke, all paine the mind forbeares,
    or on the earth no fierie sprits may moue,
    that eyes weepe worse then hart in bloody teares,
    that sence feeles more thē what doth sence cōtaine.
No, no, she is too wise, shee knowes her face
    hath not such paine as it makes Louers haue:
    shee knowes the sicknes of that perfect place
    hath yet such health as it my life can saue.
But this shee thinks, our paines hie cause excuseth,
Where her who should rule paine, false paine abuseth.
                             Since

SONNET. VI.

S Ince ſhunning paine, I eaſe can neuer finde,
  ſince baſhful dread ſeeks wher he knows me harmd
  ſince will is wonne, and ſtopped eares are charmd,
  ſince force doth faint, & ſight doth make me blind
Since looſing long, the faſter ſtill I binde,
  ſince naked ſence can conquer reaſon armde,
  ſince hart in chilling feare with Ice is warmd
  in fine, ſince ſtrife of thought but marrs the mind,
Iyeeld (ô Loue) vnto thy loathed yoke.
  Yet crauing law of armes, whoſe rule doth teach,
  that hardly vſd who euer pryſon broke,
  in iuſtice quit of honor made no breach :
Whereas if I a gratefull Gardian haue,
Thou art my Lord, and I thy vowed ſlaue.

                                        When

SONNET. VII.

WHen Loue puft vp with rage of hie difdaine,
  resolu'd to make mee patterne of his might,
  like foe whofe wit's inclind to deadly fpight,
  would often kill to breede more feeling paine.
·He would not armde with beautie onely raigne,
  on thofe affects that eafely yeeld to fight :
  but vertue fets fo hie, that reafons light
  for all his ftrife can onely bondage gaine ;
So that I liue to pay a mortall fee,
  dead-palfey ficke of all my chiefeft parts,
  like thofe whom dreames make ougly monfters fee,
  and cry, ô helpe, with naught but grones & ftarts.
Longing to haue, hauing no will to wifh,
To ftammering minds fuch is good *Cupids* difh.

                                    In

SONNET. VIII.

IN wonted walkes since wonted fancies change,
   some cause there is which of strange cause doth rise :
   for in each thing whereto mine eye doth range,
   part of my paine mee seemes ingraued lies.
The rocks which were of constant minds the marke,
   in climbing steepe, now hard refusall shoe :
   the shadie woods seeme now my sunne to darke,
   and stately hills disdaine to looke so low.
The restfull caues, now restlesse visions giue,
   in dales I see each way a hard assent :
   like late mowne meades, late cut from ioy I liue,
   alas, sweet Brookes doe in my teares augment.
Rocks, woods, hils, caues, dales, meades, brooks answer
Infected mindes infect each thing they see.   (mee,
                                 Woe

SONNET. IX.

WOe to mine eyes, the organs of mine ill,
    hate to my hart for not concealing ioy,
    a double curse vpon my tongue be still,
    whose babling lost what els I might enioy.
When first mine eyes did with thy beautie toy,
    they to my hart thy wondrous vertues told,
    who fearing least thy beames should him destroy,
    what ere he knew did to my tongue vnsold.
My teltale tongue, in talking ouer bold,
    what they in priuate counsell did declare,
    to thee in plaine and publique tearmes vnrould,
    and so by that made thee more coyer farre.
What in thy praise he spoake, that didst thou trust,
And yet my sorrowes thou doost hold vniust.

                                        Of

SONNET. X.

OF an Athenian youngman haue I red,
   who on blind Fortunes picture doted so,
   that when he could not buy it to his bed,
   on it he gazing died so very wo.
My Fortunes picture art thou flintie Dame,
   that settest golden apples to my sight,
   but wilt by no meanes let mee taste the same:
   to drowne in sight of land is double spight.
Of Fortune as thou learn'dst to be vnkind,
   so learne to be vnconstant to disdaine:
   the wittiest women are to sport inclind,
   honor is pride, and pride is naught but paine.
Let others boast of choosing for the best,
Tis substances, not names must make vs blest.

                      The

The fourth Decad.

SONNET. I.

NEedes must I leaue, and yet needes must I loue,
  in vaine my wit doth tell in verse my woe,
dispaire in me disdaine in thee doth shoe,
how by my wit I doe my folly proue :
All this my hart from loue can neuer moue.
  loue is not in my hart, no Lady no,
  my hart is loue it selfe, till I forgoe
  my hart, I neuer can my loue remoue.
How can I then leaue loue ? I doe intend
  not to craue grace, but yet to wish it still.
  Not to praise thee, but beauty to commend,
  and so by beauties praise, praise thee I will.
For as my hart is loue, loue not in mee,
So beauty thou, beauty is not in thee.

                                    Sweete

SONNET. II.

SWeete Soueraigne, sith so many minds remaine
  obedient subiects at thy beauties call,
    so many harts bound in thy haires as thrall,
    so many eyes die with one lookes disdaine,
Goe seeke the horsour that doth thee pertaine,
    that the fist Monarchie may thee befall.
    Thou hast such meanes to conquer men withall,
    as all the world must yeeld, or els be slaine.
To fight, thou need'st no weapons but thine eyes,
    thine haire hath gold enough to pay thy men,
    and for their foode, thy beauty will suffise.
    For men and armour, (Lady) care haue none,
For one will sooner yeeld vnto thee then
When he shall meete thee naked all alone.

                      When

SONNET. III.

WHen your perfections to my thoughts appeare,
　　they say among themselues ; ò happy wee,
　which euer shall so rare an obiect see :
　but happy hart, if thoughts lesse happy were,
For their delights haue cost my hart full deere,
　　in whom of loue a thousand causes be,
　and each cause breedes a thousand loues in me,
　and each loue more then thousand harts can beare.
How can my hart so many loues then hold,
　　which yet (by heapes) increase from day to day ?
　but like a shyp that's ouer-charg'd with gold,
　must either sinke, or hurle the gold away.
But hurle not loue : thou canst not feeble hart.
In thine owne blood, thou therefore drowned art.

　　　　　　D 1.　　　　　　Fooles

SONNET. IIII.

FOoles be they that inueigh gainſt Mahomet,
  who's but a morrall of loues Monarchie :
  by a dull Adamant, as ſtraw by Iet,
  he in an yron cheſt was drawne on hie.
In midſt of *Mecas* temple roofe, ſome ſay,
  he now hangs, without touch or ſtay at all ;
  That Mahomet is ſhee to whom I pray,
  (may nere man pray ſo vneffectuall.)
Mine eyes, loues ſtrange exhaling Adamants,
  vnwares to my harts temples height haue raught
  the yron Idoll that compaſſion wants,
  who my oft teares and trauels ſets at naught.
Iron hath beene tranſ-formd to gold by arte,
Her face, lymmes, fleſh, and all gold, ſaue her hart.

                           Ready

SONNET. V.

REady to ſeeke out death, in my diſgrace
　my Miſtres gan to ſmooth her gathered browes,
　whereby I am repriued for a ſpace :
　ô Hope & Feare, who halfe your tormēts knowes?
It is ſome mercie in a black-mouth'd Iudge,
　to haſte his pryſoners end, if he muſt die.
Deere, if all other fauour you ſhall grudge,
　doe ſpeedie execution with your eye.
With one ſole looke, you leaue in me no ſoule,
　count it a loſſe to loſe a faithfull ſlaue;
　would God that I might heare my laſt bell toule,
　ſo in your boſome I might dig my graue.
Doubtfull delay is worſe then any feuer,
Or helpe me ſoone, or caſt me off for euer.

SONNET. VI.

E Ach day new proofes of newe difpaire I finde,
  that is, newe deathes : no maruell then though I
make exile my laft helpe; to th'end mine eye
fhould not behold the death to me affignd.
Not that from death abfence might faue my minde,
  but that it might take death more patiently :
like him the which by Iudge condemnd to die,
to fuffer with more eafe, his eyes doth blind.
Your lippes (in fcarlet clad) my Iudges be,
  pronouncing fentence of eternall no !
Difpaire the hangman that tormenteth me,
  the death I fuffer, is the life I haue;
For onely life doth make me die in woe,
And onely death I for my pardon craue.

                      The

SONNET. VII.

THE richest relique *Rome* did euer view,
  was *Cæsars* tombe, on which with cunning hand
  Ioues tryple honours the three faire Graces stande,
  telling his vertues in their vertues true.
This *Rome* admir'd : but deerest Deere, in you
  dwelleth the wonder of the happiest land,
  And all the world to *Neptunes* furthest strand.
  For what *Rome* shapt; hath liuing life in you.
Thy naked beautie bounteously displaid,
  enricheth monarchies of harts with loue,
  thine eares to heare complaints are open laid :
  thine eyes kind lookes, requite all paines I proue,
That of my death I dare not thee accuse,
But pryde in me that baser chaunce refuse.

D. 3

Why

SONNET. VIII.

WHy thus vniustly, say my cruell fate,
    doost thou adiudge my lucklesse eyes and hart ?
    The one to liue exild from that sweet smart
    where th'other pines, imprisond without date.
My lucklesse eyes must neuer more debate,
    of those bright beames that easd my loue apart :
    and yet my hart, bound to them with loues dart,
    must there dwell euer, to bemone my state.
O had mine eyes beene suffred there to rest,
    often they had my harts vnquiet easd,
    or had my hart with banishment been blest,
    mine eye with beautie neuer had beene pleasd ;
But since these crosse effects hath fortune wrought,
Dwell hart with her, eyes view her in my thought.

                            Oft

SONNET. IX.

Oft haue I mus'd, but now at length I finde,
    why thofe that die, men fay they doe depart ;
depart a word fo gentle to my minde,
    weakely did feeme to paint deaths ougly dart.
But now the ftars, with their ftrange courfe do binde
    mee one to leaue, with whom I leaue my hart.
I heare a cry of fpyrits faint and blind,
    that parting thus, my cheefeft part I part.
Part of my life, the loathed part to mee,
    liues to impart my wearie day-fome breath ;
    but that good part wherein all comforts be,
    now dead, doe fhow departure is a death.
Yea worfe then death, death parts both woe & ioy,
From ioy I part, ftill liuing in annoy.

Hope

SONNET. X.

HOpe, like the *Hyenna* comming to be old,
  alters his shape, is turn'd into dispaire :
  pitty my hoarie hopes, maid of cleere mould,
  thinke not that frownes can euer make thee faire.
What harme is it to kisse, to laugh, to play ?
  Beauties no blossome if it be not vs'd,
  sweet daliance keepeth wrinkles long away,
  repentance followes them that haue refus'd.
To bring you to the knowledge of your good,
  I seeke, I sue, ô try and then beleeue,
  each Image can be chast thats caru'd of wood :
  you show you liue when men you doe releeue.
Iron with wearing shines, rust wasteth treasure,
On earth but loue there is no other pleasure.

                           The

The fifth Decad.

SONNET. I.

AYe mee poore wretch, my prayer is turnd to sinne,
  I say I loue, my Mistres saies tis lust :
  thus most wee loose, where most wee seeke to win,
  wit will make wicked what is nere so iust.
And yet I can supplant her false surmise.
  Lust is a fire, that for an howre or twaine
  gyueth a scorching blaze, and then he dies.
  Loue, a continuall fornace doth maintaine.
A fornace, well this a fornace may be call'd,
  for it burnes inward, yeelds a smothering flame,
  sighes which like boyld leads smoking vapor scald.
  I sigh a pace at eccho of sighes name.
Long haue I seru'd, no short blaze is my loue,
Hid ioyes there are that maydes scorne till they proue.

                                 I

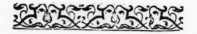

SONNET. II.

I Doe not now complaine of my difgrace,
 ô cruell fayre one, fayre with cruell croft :
 nor of the hower, feafon, time nor place,
 nor of my foyle for any freedom loft ;
Nor of my courage by mif-fortune daunted,
 nor of my wit, by ouer-weening ftrooke,
 nor of my fence, by any founde inchaunted,
 nor of the force of fierie poynted hooke.
Nor of the fteele that fticks within my wound,
 nor of my thoughts, by worfer thoughts defac'd,
 nor of the life I labour to confound ;
 But I complaine, that beeing thus difgrac'd,
Fyerd, feard, frantick, fetterd, fhot through, flaine,
My death is fuch as I may not complaine.

            If

SONNET: III.

IF euer sorrow spoke from soule that loues,
  as speakes a spirit in a man possest,
    in mee her spirit speakes, my soule it moues,
    whose sigh-swolne words breed whirlwinds in my
Or like the eccho of a passing bell,   (brest.
    which sounding on the water, seemes to howle :
    so rings my hart a feareful heauie knell,
    and keepes all night in consort with the Owle.
My cheekes with a thin Ice of teares is clad,
    mine eyes like morning starres are bleer'd and red:
    what resteth then but I be raging mad,
    to see that shee, (my cares cheefe conduit head)
When all streames els help quench my burning hart,
Shuts vp her springs, and will no grace impart.

                                             You

SONNET. IIII.

YOu secrete vales, you solitarie fieldes,
  you shores forsaken, and you sounding rocks :
if euer groning hart hath made you yeeld,
  or words halfe spoke that sence in prison locks,
Then mongst night shadowes whisper out my death;
  that when my selfe hath seald my lips frō speaking,
each tell-tale eccho with a weeping breath,
  may both record my trueth, & true loues breaking.
You prettie flowers that smile for Sommers sake,
  pull in your heads before my watrie eyes
  doe turne the Medowes to a standing lake :
  by whose vntimely floodes your glory dies.
For loe, mine hart resolu'd to moystning ayre,
Feedeth mine eyes, which doubles teare for teare.

His

SONNET. V.

His shadow to *Narcissus* well presented
how faire hee was by such attracting loue :
so if thou would'st thy selfe thy beauty proue,
vulgar breath-myrrors might haue wel contented,
And to theyr prayers eternally consented.
　Othes, vowes, & sighes, if they beliefe might moue,
　but more thou forst, making my pen aproue
　thy praise to all, least any had disented.
With this hath wrought, y̌ which before wert known
　but vnto some, of all art now required,
　& thine eies wonders wrong'd, because not shown
the world, with daily orizons desired.
Thy chast faire gifts, with learnings breath is blowne,
And thus my pen hath made thy sweetes admired.

I

SONNET. VI.

I Am no modell figure, or figne of care,
  but his eternall harts confuming effence,
  in whom griefes comentaries written are,
  drawing groffe paffion into pure quinteffence.
Not thine eyes fire, but fire of thine eyes difdaine,
  fed by neglect of my continuall greeuing,
  attracts the true liues fpirit of my paine,
  and giues it thee, which giues mee no releeuing.
Within thine armes fad Eligies I fing,
  vnto thine eyes a true hart loue torne lay I,
  thou fmell'ft from me the fauours forrowes bring,
  my teares to taft my trueth, to touch difplay I.
Loe thus each fence (deere faire one) I importune,
But beeing care, thou flyeft mee as ill fortune.

                                  But

SONNET. VII.

BVt beeing care, thou flyeſt mee as ill fortune.
Care the conſuming canker of the mind,
the diſcord that diſorders ſweet harts tune,
th'abortiue baſtard of a coward mind :
The light-foote lackie that runnes poſt by death,
bearing the Letters which containe our end,
the buſie aduocate that ſells his breath,
denouncing worſt to him is moſt his friend.
O Deere, this care no intreſt holdes in mee,
but holy care, the Gardian of thy faire,
thine honors champion, and thy vertues ſee,
the zeale w͂ thee from barbarus times ſhall beare.
This care am I, this care my life hath taken,
Deere to my ſoule, then leaue me not forſaken.

Deere

SONNET. VIII.

D Eere to my soule, then leaue me not forsaken,
   flie not, my hart within thy bosome sleepeth :
euen from my selfe and sence I haue betaken
mee vnto thee, for whom my spirit weepeth.
And on the shoare of that salt tedrie sea,
   couch'd in a bed of vnseene seeming pleasure,
where, in imaginarie thoughts thy faire selfe lay,
   but being wakt, robd of my liues best treasure.
I call the heauens, ayre, earth, & seas, to heare
   my loue, my trueth, and black disdaind estate :
beating the rocks with bellowings of dispaire,
   which stil with plaints my words reuerbarate.
Sighing, alas, what shall become of me ?
Whilst Eccho cryes, what shal become of me.

                             Whilst

SONNET. IX.

Whilst Eccho cryes, what shall become of mee,
  and desolate my desolations pitty,
thou in thy beauties charrack sitt'st to see
my tragick down-fall, and my funerall ditty.
No Tymbrell, but my hart thou pay'st vpon,
  whose strings are stretch'd vnto the hiest key,
  the dyopazon loue, loue is the vnison,
in loue, my life and labours wast away.
Onely regardlesse, to the world thou leau'st mee,
  whilst slaine-hopes, turning frō the feast of sorrow,
vnto Dispaire (their King) which nere deceiues me,
  captiues my hart, whose blacke night hates ẙ mor-
And hee, in ruth of my distressed cry,   (row.
Plants mee a weeping starre within mine eye.

E 1

Prome-

SONNET. X.

PRometheus, for stealing liuing fire
   from heauens King, was iudg'd eternall death,
   in selfe same flame with vnrelenting ire,
   bound fast to *Caucasus* lowe foote beneath.
So I, for stealing liuing beauties fire
   into my verse, that it may alwaies liue,
   and change his formes to shapes of thy desire,
   thou beauties Queene, selfe sentence like dost giue.
Bound to thy feete, in chaines of loue I lie,
   for to thine eyes I neuer dare aspire,
   and in thy beauties brightnes doe I fry,
   as poore *Prometheus* in the scalding fire.
Which teares maintaine, as oyle the Lampe reuiues,
Onely my succour in thy fauour lyes.

The.

The sixth Decad.

SONNET. I.

ONe Sunne vnto my liues day giues true light,
　one Moone disolues my stormie night of woes,
One starre my fate and happy fortune shoes,
One Saint I serue, one shrine with vowes I dight.
One Sunne transfixt hath burnt my hart out-right,
　one Moone oppos'd, my loue in darknes throes,
　one star hath bid my thoughts my wrongs disclose,
　Saints scorne poore swaines, shrines doe my vowes
Yet if my loue be found a holy fier,　　　(no right.
　pure, vnstain'd, without Idolatrie,
　and shee naythlesse, in hate of my desire,
　liues to repose her in my miserie.
My sunne, my moone, my star, my saint, my shrine,
Mine be the torment, but the guilt be thine.

SONNET. II.

TO liue in hell, and heauen to behold,
  to welcome life, and die a liuing death,
  to sweat with heate, and yet be freezing cold,
  to graspe at starres, and lye the earth beneath ;
To tread a Maze that neuer shall haue end,
  to burne in sighes, and starue in daily teares,
  to clime a hill, and neuer to discend,
  Gyants to kill, and quake at childish feares ;
To pyne for foode, and watch Thesperian tree,
  to thirst for drinke, and Nectar still to draw,
  to liue accurst, whom men hold blest to be,
  and weepe those wrongs which neuer creature saw,
If this be loue, if loue in these be founded,
My hart is loue, for these in it are grounded.

A

SONNET. III.

A Carver, hauing lou'd too-long in vaine,
  hewed out the portrature of *Venus* sonne
  in Marble rocke, vpon the which did raine
  small drizling drops, that from a fount did runne.
Imagining, the drops would eyther weare
  his furie out, or quench his liuing flame.
  But when hee saw it bootlesse did appeare,
  hee swore the water did augment the same.
So, I that seeke in verse to carue thee out,
  hoping thy beauty will my flame alay,
  viewing my verse and Poems all throughout,
  find my will, rather to my loue obey.
That, with the Caruer, I my worke doe blame,
Finding it still th'augmentor of my flame.

E 3

Astro-

SONNET. IIII.

Astronomers the heauens doe deuide,
   into eight Houses, where the Gods remaines,
   all which in thy perfections doe abide,
   for in thy feete, the Queene of silence raignes,
About thy wast, *Ioues* messenger doth dwell,
   inchaunting mee as I thereat admire :
   and on thy duggs, the Queene of loue doth tell
   her god-heads power, in scrowles of my desire.
Thy beautie, is the worlds eternall Sunne,
   thy fauours force a cowards hart to darre,
   and in thy hayres, *Ioue* and his riches wunne ;
   thy frownes hold *Saturne*, thine eyes ÿ fixed stars.
Pardon mee then diuine to loue thee well,
Since thou art heauen, and I in heauen would dwell.
                        Wearie

SONNET. V.

WEarie of loue, my thoughts of loue complaind,
till Reaſon told them there was no ſuch power,
and bad mee view faire beauties richeſt flower,
to ſee if there a naked boy remaind.
Deere to thine eyes, eyes that my ſoule hath paind,
thoughts turn'd them back in that vnhappy hower
to ſee if Loue keepe there his royall bower,
for if not there, then no place him containd.
There was hee not, nor boy, nor golden bow,
yet as thou turnd thy chaſt faire eye aſide,
a flame of fire did from thine eye lyds goe,
w̄ burnt my hart through my fore wounded ſide.
Then with a ſigh, reaſon made thoughts to cry,
There is no God of loue, ſaue that thine eye.

For-

SONNET. VI.

FOrgiue mee Deere, for thundring on thy name,
  sith tis thy selfe that showes my loue distrest,
  for fire exhald, in freezing clowdes possest,
  warring for way, makes all the heauens exclaime.
Thy beautie so, the brightest liuing flame,
  wrapt in my clowdie hart by winter prest,
  scorning to dwell within so base a nest,
  thunders in mee thine euerlasting fame.
O that my hart might still containe that fire,
  or that the fire would alwaies light my hart,
  then should'st thou not disdaine my true desire,
  or thinke I wrong'd thee, to reueale my smart.
For as the fire through freezing clowdes doth breake,
So, not my selfe, but thou in mee would'st speake.

My

SONNET. VII.

MY hart, mine eye accuseth of his death,
  saying, his wanton sight bred his vnrest :
Mine eye affirmes, my harts vnconstant faith
hath beene his bane, and all his ioyes represt.
My hart auowes mine eye let in the fire,
  which burnes him with an euer-liuing light,
  mine eye replyes, my greedy harts desire,
  let in those floods W drownes him day & night.
Thus warres my hart, which reason doth maintaine,
  and calls mine eye to combat if he darre :
  the whilst my soule, impatient of disdaine,
  wrings from his bondage vnto death more narre ;
Saue that my loue, still holdeth him in hand,
" A kingdome thus deuided, cannot stand.

Vnhappy

SONNET. VIII.

Vnhappy day, vnhappy month and feafon,
 when firft proud loue my ioyes away adiourning
pour'd into mine eye, (to her eye turning)
 a deadly iuyce, vnto my greene thoughts gayfon.
Pryfoner I am vnto the eye I gaze on,
 eternally my loues flame is in burning,
 a mortall fhaft ftill woudds mee in my mourning;
thus prifond, burnt & flain, ỹ fprit, ỹ foule & reafõ.
What tids me then, fince thefe paines w̃ annoy mee,
 in my difpaire are euer-more increafing?
 the more I loue, leffe is my paines releafing,
 that curfed be the fortune which deftroyes me.
The hower, the month, the feafon and the caufe,
When loue firft made me thrall to louers lawes.
          Loue

SONNET. IX.

Oue haue I followed al too-long naught gaining,
and sigh'd I haue in vaine to sweet what smarteth,
but from his bow a fiery arrow parteth,
thinking that I should him resist, not playning.
But cowardly my hart submisse remaining,
yeelds to receiue what shaft thy faire eye darteth :
well doe I see thine eye, my bale imparteth,
and that saue death no hope I am detaining.
For what is he can alter Fortunes slyding ?
one in his bed consumes his life away,
other in warres, another in the sea,
the like effects in mee haue theyr abiding.
For heauens avowed my fortune shonld be such,
That I should die by louing farre too much.

 My

SONNET. X.

MY God, my God, how much I loue my goddesse,
whose vertues rare, vnto the heauens arise,
my God, my God, how much I loue her eyes,
one shining bright, the other full of hardnes.
My God, my God, how much I loue her wisdome,
whose words may rauish heauens richest Maker,
of whose eyes-ioyes, if I might be pertaker,
then to my soule a holy rest would come.
My God, how much I loue to heare her speake,
whose hands I kisse, & rauisht oft rekisseth,
whē she stands wotlesse whō so much she blisseth.
Say then what mind this honest loue wold breake,
Since her perfections pure withouten blot,
Makes her belou'd of them shee knoweth not?

The

The seauenth Decad.

SONNET. I.

THE first created, held a ioyous bower,
  a flowring fielde, the worlds sole wonderment,
  hyght Paradise, from whence a womans power,
  entic'd him fall to endlesse banishment.
This, on the banks of *Euphrates* did stand,
  till the first Moouer by his wondrous might,
  planted it in thine eyes, thy face, thy hands,
  from whence the world receiues his fairest light.
Thy cheeks cōtaines choice flowers, thy eyes two suns,
  thy hands the fruite that no life blood can staine,
  and in thy breath, that heauenly musick wons,
  which whē y̆ speak'st, Angels their voyces straines.
As from the first, thy sexe exiled mee,
So to this next, let mee be call'd by thee.

                                Fayre

SONNET. II.

FAyre Grace of Graces, Muse of Muses all,
   thou Paradise, thou onely heauen I know,
   what influence hath bred my hateful woe,
   that I from thee and them am forst to fall?
Thou falne from mee, from thee I neuer shall,
   although my fortunes thou hast brought so loe,
   yet shall my faith and seruice with thee goe,
   for liue I doe, on heauen and thee to call.
Banisht all grace, no Graces with mee dwell,
   compeld to muse, why Muses from mee flye,
   excluded heauen, what can remaine but hell?
   exil'd from Paradise, in hate I lye.
Cursing my starres, albe I find it true,
I lost all these when I lost loue and you.

What

SONNET. III.

What view'd I deere when I thine eyes beheld ?
  Loue in his glory ? no, him *Thyrsis* saw,
  and stoode the boy, whilst hee his darts did draw,
  whose painted pride to baser swaines he tell'd.
Saw I two sunnes ? that sight is seene but seld,
  yet can their broode that teach the holy law
  gaze on their beames, and dread them not a straw,
  where princely lookes are by their eyes repeld.
What saw I then ? doubtlesse it was Amen,
  arm'd with strong thunder & a lightnings flame,
  who bridgroome like, with power was riding than
  meaning that none should see him when he came.
Yet did I gaze, and thereby caught the wound
Which burnes my hart, and keepes my body sound.
                              When

SONNET. IIII.

WHen tedious much, and ouer-wearie long,
  cruell disdaine, reflecting from her brow,
hath beene the cause that I endur'd such wrong,
and rest thus discontent, and wearie now.
Yet when posteritie in time to come,
  shall finde th'vncanceld tenor of her vow,
and her disdaine be then confest of some,
how much vnkind, and long I finde it now.
O yet euen then, (though then will be too late
  to comfort mee, dead many a day ere then)
they shall confesse I did not force her hart,
  and tyme shall make it knowne to other men,
That nere had her disdaine made mee dispaire,
Had she not beene so excellently faire.

                            Had

SONNET. V.

Had shee not beene so excellently faire,
   my Muse had neuer mourn'd in lines of woe,
   but I did too too inestimable wey her,
   and that's the cause I now lament me so.
Yet not for her contempt doe I complaine mee,
   (complaints may ease the minde, but that is all,)
   therefore though shee too constantly disdaine mee
   I can but sigh and greeue, and so I shall :
Yet greeue I not, because I must greeue euer,
   and yet (alas) waste teares away in vaine.
   I am resolued, truely to perseuer,
   though shee persisteth in her olde disdaine,
But that which grieues mee most, is that I see,
Those which most faire, the most vnkindest bee.

SONNET. VI.

THus long impos'd to euerlasting plaining,
    (diuinely conftant to the worthieft Fayre)
and mooued by eternally difdayning,
aye to perfeuer in vnkind defpayre:
Becaufe now, Silence, wearily confinde
in tedious dying: and a dombe reftraint,
Breakes forth in teares from mine vnable mind,
to eafe her paffion by a poore complaint.
O doe not therefore to thy felfe fuggeft
that I can greeue, to haue immur'd fo long.
Vpon the matter of mine owne vnreft:
fuch greete is not the tenor of my fong,
that hyde fo zealoufly fo bad a wrong.
My greefe is this: vnleffe I fpeake and plaine mee,
Thou wilt perfeuer, euer to difdaine mee

                                        Thou

SONNET. VII.

THou wilt perseuer, euer to disdaine mee,
   and I shall then dye, when thou wilt repent it :
   ô doe not therefore from complaint restraine mee,
   and take my life from mee, to mee that lent it.
For whilst these accents, weepingly exprest
   in humble lynes, of reuerentest zeale,
   Haue issue to complaint, from mine vnrest
   they but thy beauties wonder shall reueale.
And though the greeued Muse, of some other *Louer*,
   (whose lesse deuotions knew but woes like mine)
   would rather seeke occasion to discouer,
   how little pittifull, and how much vnkind,
   they other (not so worthy beauties) find.
O I not so, bnt seeke with humble prayer,
Meanes how to mooue th'vnmercifullest fayre.

SONNET. VIII.

AS drawes the golden Meteor of the day,
　Exhaled matter from the ground, to heauen,
　and by his secret nature, there doth stay
　the thing fast held, and yet of hold bereauen,
So by th'attractiue excellence, and might,
　borne to the power of thy transparant eyes,
　drawne from my selfe, rauisht with thy delight,
　whose dumbe conceits diuinely syranyze :
Loe ; in suspence of feare, and hope, vpholden,
　diuersly poyz'd, with passions that paine mee,
　no resolution dares my thoughts imbolden,
　since tis not I, but thou that doost sustaine mee.
O if ther's none but thou can worke my woe,
Wilt thou be still vnkind and kill mee so ?

Wilt

SONNET. IX.

Wilt thou be still vnkind and kill mee so?
 whose humbled vowes, with sorrowful apeale,
 doe still persist, and did so long agoe
 intreate for pitty, with so pure a zeale ?
Suffise the world shall, (for the world can say)
 How much thy power hath power, & what it can,
 neuer was victor-hand yet moou'd to slay
 the rendred captiue, or the yeelding man.
Then ô : why should thy woman-thought impose
 death and disdaine on him that yeelds his breath,
 to free his soule, from discontent, and woes :
 and humble sacrifice to a certaine death ?
O since the world knowes, what the power can doe,
What wert for thee to saue and loue mee to ?

SONNET. X.

I Mete not mine, by others difcontent,
   for none compares with mee in true deuotion,
   yet though my teares and fighes to her be fpent,
   her cruell hart difdaines what they doe motion,
Yet though perfifting in eternall hate,
   to agrauate the caufe of my complayning,
   her furie nere confineth with a date,
   I will not ceafe to loue for her difdaining.
Such punie thoughts of vnrefolued ground,
   whofe inaudacitie dares but bafe conceite,
   in mee, and my loue, neuer fhall be found ;
   thofe coward thoughts vnworthy minds awaite :
But thofe that loue well, haue not yet begun,
Perfeuer euer, and haue neuer done.

Perfeuer

The eyght Decad.

SONNET. I.

PErſeuer euer, and haue neuer done.
　You weeping accent of my weatie ſong,
　O doe not you eternall paſſions ſhunne,
　but be you true, and euerlaſting long.
Say that ſhee doth requite you with diſdaine,
　yet fortified with hope, endure your foreune :
　though cruell now, ſhee will be kinde againe,
　ſuch haps as thoſe, ſuch loues as yours importune:
Though ſhee proteſts the faithfulleſt ſeueritie,
　inexecrable beautie is inflicting :
　Kindneſſe (in time) will pitty your ſinceroty,
　though now it be your fortunes interdicting.
For ſom can ſay, whoſe loues haue known like paſſiõ,
Women are kind by kind, and coy for faſhon.
　　　　　　　　　　　　　　　Giue

SONNET. II.

Giue Period to my matter of complaining,
    faire wonder of our times admiring eye :
    and entertaine no more thy long difdaining.
    Or giue mee leaue (at laft) that I may dye.
For who can-lyue, perpetually fecluded
    from death to life, that loathes her difcontent ?
    Leffe by fome hope feducingly deluded,
    fuch thoughts afpyre to fortunate euent :
But I, that nowe haue drawne Mal-pleafant breath,
    vnder the burden of thy cruell hate,
    ô I muft long, and linger after death,
    and yet I dare not giue my life her date.
For if I dye, and thou repent t'haue flaine mee,
T'wil griue mee more then if thou did'ft difdaine me.
                                                    T'will

SONNET. III.

T'will grieue me more thē if thou didst disdaine me,
   that I should die, and thou because I dye so :
   and yet to die, it should not know to paine me,
   if cruell Beauty were content to bid so
Death, to my life : life, to my long dispaire,
   prolong'd by her : giuen to my loue and dayes :
   are meanes to tell how truely she is faire,
   and I can die to testifie her praise :
Yet not to die though fairenes mee despiseth,
   is cause why in complaint I thus perseuer,
   though Death mee and my loue imparadizeth,
   by interdicting mee, from her for euer :
I doe not greeue that I am forst to die,
But die, to thinke vpon the reason, Why.

                              My

SONNET. IIII.

MY teares are true, though others be diuine,
   and sing of warres, and *Troys* new-rising frame,
   meeting Heroick feete in euery line,
   that tread high measures on the Scene of Fame.
And I though disaccustoming my Muse,
   and sing but low songs in an humble vaine,
   may one day raise my stile as others vse,
   and turne *Elizon* to a higher straine.
When reintombing from oblius ages,
   in better stanzas her suruiuing wonder,
   I may oppos'd against the monster-rages
   that part desert, and excellence a sunder :
That shee, (though coy) may yet suruiue to see
Her beauties wonder lyues againe in mee.

                        Some.

SONNET. V.

S Omtimes in verse I prais'd, somtime in verse I sight,
  no more shal pen with loue and beauty mell,
  but to my hart alone, my hart shall tell,
  how vnseene flames doe burne it day and night.
Least flames giue light, light brings my loue to sight,
  and my loue proue my follie to excell.
  wherefore my loue burnes like the fire of hell,
  wherein is fire, and yet there is no light.
For if one neuer lou'd like mee, then why
  skillesse blames hee the thing hee doth not know?
  and hee that so hath lou'd should fauour show,
  for hee hath beene a foole as well as I.
Thus shall hence-forth more paine more folly haue,
And folly past, may iustly pardon craue.

A

A calculation vpon the birth of an honourable
Ladies daughter, borne in the yeere,
1 5 8 8. and on a Friday.

FAyre by inheritance ; whom borne wee see,
both in the wondrous yeere, and on the day
wherein the fairest Planet beareth sway :
the heauens to thee this fortune doe decree.
Thou of a world of harts in time shalt be
a Monarch great, and with one beauties ray
so many hoasts of harts thy face shall slay,
as all the rest (for loue) shall yeeld to thee.
But euen as *Alexander* (when he knewe
his Fathers conquests) wept, least he should leaue
no Kingdome vnto him for to subdue :
so shall thy mother thee of praise bereaue.
So many harts already shee hath slaine,
As few behind to conquer shall remaine.

FINIS.